Apple TV 4K|HD Hacl

Ultimate List of the Essential Tips and Tricks

Bonus: 87 Siri Commands

written by Nathan Richardson

INTRODUCTION

I wrote this book after owning the Apple TV 4K for some time and I strongly believe that everybody should get to know all the interesting features (or at least almost all the ones I know of) that can make your life significantly easier. I would like to briefly express my gratitude that you are reading these lines. It means a lot to me.

This book is not exhaustingly long, but I believe it is packed with the most relevant and useful information on the topic. In case anything is not true or functional, please do not hesitate to send me an email at nathan.richardson.co@gmail.com.

I am also using this opportunity to express my gratitude to everyone who has supported me through the writing process and through my entire life. I am thankful to my wife, parents and colleagues for their inspiring guidance and friendly advice which helped in the process of writing this book.

That's enough, I suppose, so let's start with the best tricks and the most interesting features right now!

Table of Contents

How to Pair Bluetooth Headphones

Fortunately, your Apple TV supports all kinds of Bluetooth accessories. You can without worries connect keyboards, wireless headphones, game controllers and beyond to your Apple TV. Simply put the accessory in pairing mode and then head into Settings > Remotes and Devices > Bluetooth > tap on the accessory you want to pair. Enter required pairing pin. So, let's start and pair your AirPods to your TV.

How to Perform Reboot

There are two ways how to perform a system reboot. You can do it in the Settings but doing it via Siri remote is probably easier. To do that, hold down the Home and Menu buttons on the Siri remote control at the same time until the light on the front of the Apple TV starts blinking. Then simply let go of the buttons and the TV should reboot.

How to Keep Multiple TVs in Sync

Do you own more than one Apple TV, and would you like to have same apps and options across all your devices?

Luckily, you can activate Home Screen which will automatically sync all your apps, folders etc.

To activate One Home Screen, head into Settings > Accounts > iCloud > switch on One Home Screen to On.

What Happens If You Say Famous Movie Quote

If you say a famous movie quote, Siri can find the movie it came from. Try telling Siri "may the force be with you," and wait for the result.

Why to Learn Siri Remote Shortcuts

Apple TV's Siri Remote maybe looks basic but every button has a double-click and a touch-and-hold action. Would you like to learn these actions?

- Quickly view list of available audio outputs by holding the Play/Pause button. Then you can select different output.

- Switch between apps (or rather enter the App Switcher) by double-clicking the Home/TV button

- Enable instantly screensaver by pressing the Menu button while being on the Home screen

- Tap once on the touchpad and reveal the scrubber with the current timestamp. Tap once again and the timestamps will change to the current time and the end time

How to Disable TV App Shortcut

You have probably already noticed that when you tap on the home button it will take you to the TV app.

If you want to change that, head into Settings > Remotes and Devices > Home button and tap on Home Screen.

How to Enable AirPlay Security

Apple TV has built-in AirPlay compatibility which allows you to watch content from your phone or tablet on your TV. To restrict access to your Apple TV head into Settings > AirPlay and choose who will have access to your TV screen. Moreover, you can even require PIN for successful connection.

In case you have older device head into Settings > AirPlay > Security to set a verification code or a password.

How to Set Parental Restrictions

Would you like to prevent your children from watching at certain TV shows, movies, etc.? Simply head into Settings > General > Restrictions and set a four-digit code to enable this feature.

You can completely block the ability to make purchases and access explicit content. Naturally, you can as well filter TV, movies, music, and podcasts based on language, ratings, or age.

How to Share Media Content with Family Members

It would be wasteful if the family members would be forced to buy the same content more than once so you can access shared movies, TV shows, and apps. Head into Movies, TV Shows, or App Store, then tap on Purchased >

Family Sharing. Ultimately, select your family member to see their saved content.

How to Backspace and Access to Alternate Characters

When you are using Apple TV's onscreen keyboard and when you make a mistake, you do not have to select the backspace key. Simply, swipe left on the TV's remote touch surface and automatically delete the last letter

To access alternate characters, click down on the touch surface and hold until the alternate characters appears.

How to Watch Live TV

Streaming apps can be great, but if you wish to watch standard TV hold down the mic icon on the remote and ask to watch a channel live. Siri is quite clever and can understand if you search for a specific sporting event, try to ask for example "When are the New York Rangers playing?"

How to Use Phone as Keyboard

Would you like to save some time and type on your phone instead typing on the TV itself?

To do that:

- Connect your iPhone to the same Wi-Fi network as your TV

- Click on an empty text box on your Apple TV with your remote control

- You will see a notification on your phone that you can type via your phone

How to Browse Pictures from Your iPhone

Thanks to connection between Apple TV and your iPhone it is quite easy to see all the pictures that you took by your iPhone right on your Apple TV. To enable this feature:

- Head into Settings on your iPhone

- Click on your name at the top

- Choose iCloud

- Activate "iCloud Photos"

- Activate "Upload to My Photo Stream"

- Head into Settings on your TV

- Select Accounts

- Click on iCloud

- Head into "Photos," select "iCloud Photos" and switch it to "On"

Lastly, open the Photos app on your TV and log in to iCloud. You should see all the photos you took, and it will be updated if you take new photos.

How to Log in to Your Cable Provider

Do you know about your Apple TV's feature called Zero Sign-on? Basically, it means that if you have a cable provider, you do not need to log in to every premium app that's based on your cable subscription.

To enable Zero Sign-on:

- Head into Settings on your TV

- Select Accounts

- Choose TV Provider

- Tap on your cable provider

- Open an app that requires cable connection

- Choose "Allow" when you get a notification if you want to use your subscription

- Go to the website listed and enter in your activation code

- That is all

How to Mirror Your Phone Display

If you would to view your photos on a big screen of your TV, play videos or giving a presentation, you need to use feature called AirPlay Mirroring.

Connect both devices to the same Wi-Fi

Open Control Center on your iPhone

Open Screen Mirroring on the left

Click on Apple TV in the list of devices

Your device is now connected

How to Use Dark Mode

If you prefer dark mode to save your eyes while watching in the dark you are in luck because Apple TV supports this feature.

To enable it, head into Settings > Appearance > Dark. Automatic means that the mode will be adjusted based on time of day.

How to Access Advanced Menu

To get access at your Apple TV's advanced settings menu, head into Settings > Software Updates and tap on the Play/Pause button four times. The hidden menu can now be accessed.

If you want to set your Apple TV exactly how it would be found in an Apple Store head into Settings > General > About. Tap on the Play/Pause button four times.

How to Use Siri on Apple TV

Just hold the microphone button to speak to Siri. It is simple like that. You are going to find list of possible commands for Siri at the end of this book + you will find some Easter egg questions as well.

How to Control Your Smart Home

Who would not want to automate his or her home? Luckily it is possible with the Apple TV. To enable your TV's smart home features, head into Settings > Accounts > iCloud> switch My Home to Connected and connect your devices such as light bulbs etc.

How to Use Phone as Remote Control

If you cannot find the remote control you can simply use your iPhone, iPad, or Apple Watch as a remote. For the iPad and Apple Watch, you will need to install free Remote app. Regarding your iPhone you can simply head into Control Center and access Apple TV controls.

How to Use Universal Remote Control

You probably already have some kind of universal remote control, so you do not want to use the Siri remote control. Luckily, you can use your universal remote. To do that:

Tap on Remotes & Devices in Settings on your TV

Click on Learn Remote

Tap on Start using your universal remote.

To program your remote:

Press and hold the button you want to use the Up button on the device. Assign next six buttons in all: Up, Down, Left, Right, Select and Menu by pressing the button on the universal remote and holding it down until a progress bar is full. Then enter a name for your universal remote.

Then you will be asked to set up Play, Pause, Stop, Rewind and Fast Forward buttons. Afterwards tap on "Ok" and you are done.

How to Control Playback

Would you like to have repeated something someone said? Click the touch surface on the left to go back 10 seconds.

If you tap on the right, you will get forward 10 seconds at a time.

If you want to move through a video, pause and then swipe the trackpad in either direction to scrub back and forth. You can naturally use voice commands as well.

How to Use the App Switcher

To activate this feature, double-click on the Home button. Then you will be presented with the whole collection of recently used apps. You can use the trackpad to swipe between different apps and you can even close them by flicking them away.

How to Move and Hide Apps

Virtually all home screens become gradually cluttered. Luckily, you can move apps around, hide them, or hide them into folders.

Click and hold an app, then you can move it around the home screen. Press the Play/Pause button to hide a selected app.

To create a folder, highlight the app you want to put into a folder and hold down the touch surface for a while. Then drag it on top of another app that you want in the same folder.

If you want to create a new folder based on the highlighted app, hold it down and press Play/Pause and choose an option. Click on it to rename a folder.

How to Launch Screensavers

To force your Apple TV to show screensaver immediately head into the home screen and move to the top left corner of the screen. Tap on and hold the Menu button on the remote until the screensaver begins. Alternatively, you can double tap the home button.

How to Enable Conference Room Display Feature

Do you know that AirPlay lets you project a computer or device onto the TV? Simply put the Apple TV in Conference Room Display mode, and the TV shows a screensaver and instructions for how to connect.

To activate this feature, head into Settings > AirPlay > Conference Room Display > switch Conference Room Display to On.

How to Order Food via Apple TV

There are many apps that allow you to order food via your Apple TV. To order food:

- Launch the App Store on your TV

- Tap on "Food and Drink"

- Install some app such as GrubHub

- Visit apps website and create an account with your address and your payment info

- Log in to your account on your TV

How to Meditate with Your Apple TV

You can even meditate thanks to your Apple TV. To do that:

- Launch the App Store on your TV

- Go to the Health and Fitness category and Install Calm

- Select a meditation and relax

How to Enable Sleep Feature

Tap on and hold the Home button for 2 seconds and the Sleep option appears at the center of your screen. Tap on it and put your TV to sleep.

How to Browse Amazon

Do you know that you can browse for goods on Amazon? You can even add them to a list to buy later but you cannot buy it directly via TV. To browse for goods:

- Launch the App Store on your TV

- Install the Amazon App

- Log in to your Amazon account

- Tap on "search"

- Tap on the microphone button on your remote control and enter the search term such as "women's bags"

- Choose what you want and tap on "add to list"

How to Adjust the Trackpad's Sensitivity

You might have troubles navigating using remote trackpad. Luckily, the sensitivity is something that can be adjusted. Go to Settings > Remotes and Devices and tap on the "Touch Surface Tracking" option. Choose the sensitivity you like - Fast, Medium, or Slow.

How to Customize the Screensaver

You can actually change the screensaver and how often they update. Head into Settings > General > Screensaver > Type and select Apple Photos, Home Sharing, Music Library or My Photos. You can then change settings for every option like the frequency of updates and transitions.

How to Cancel Active Subscriptions

If you have lost track of your subscription services there is nothing easier then heading to Settings > Accounts >

Manage Subscriptions, tap on your active subscription, and cancel it immediately.

How to View Video Settings

If you are watching video on your Apple TV, you can actually access a variety of media playback settings by swiping down on your remote's touch surface. You are then presented with options such as enable/disable subtitles, change audio settings for language, sound processing, and speaker. A simple swipe up hides the overlay and returns you back to the video.

How to Switch Between Lowercase/Uppercase Keyboard

Would you like to avoid boring navigation of the cursor between the lowercase and uppercase layout? Press the Play/Pause button on your remote and it immediately switches the letters from lowercase to uppercase.

How to Delete Apps

In order to keep your home screen organized you can delete apps. To do that long press on an icon, press the Play/Pause button, tap on Delete and confirm your selection.

There is even a faster way to delete multiple apps. Head into Settings > General > Manage Storage and tap on the trash can icons to the right of the apps you want to get rid of.

Learn Hidden Menu Button Functions

The Menu button is able to perform some hidden functions. If you double-click it, the screensaver will start as you probably already know. If you click on it three times it will activate your Accessibility Shortcuts. These shortcuts contain Closed Captioning, Voice Over and for instance Zoom.

How to Install Apps Automatically

You are probably aware of the Apple feature which install apps automatically on your iPad when you install them on your iPhone. However, your Apple TV can do the same. To enable the feature, head into Settings > Apps and tap on Automatically Install Apps to activate it.

How to Control HDTV

It is obvious that there is no need to have multiple remotes when you buy Apple TV set. To be able to control your TV with the Siri remote control head into Settings > General > Remotes and Devices. First activate the Control TVs and Receivers menu. Then tap on Volume Control and select Auto.

How to Stream Music and Video with AirPlay

Your Apple TV can act as AirPlay receiver so you can even use your home theater setup as a speaker instead. To enable that click on the AirPlay icon when you are playing music or video. The icon is in the Now Playing widget on the lock screen and in the Control Center Then select your Apple TV and control the playback via Siri remote control.

How to Check Remote Control Battery Level

Is it possible to see the actual percentage of remaining battery in remote control? It is, head into Settings > Remotes and Devices to view that.

How to Reduce Loud Sounds

If you like watching TV in the night you might give a try to Reduce Loud Sounds feature. It basically volume of all loud sounds so blasts and explosions are not going to wake up your significant other. To enable that head into Settings > Video and Audio.

How to Take Screenshot

You can even record the screen of your Apple TV. To do that you must use a USB-C cable and QuickTime on your computer. Plug in the USB-C cable to the back of your TV and into your computer. Launch QuickTime and head into File > New Movie Recording. Tap on the downward-facing arrow button and select your TV from the menu.

You are going to be presented with the live preview of your TV screen. Then simply tap on the record button to start capturing the screen.

How to Connect Your HomePod

To connect your HomePod to your Apple TV, hold down the Play/Pause button on the remote control. A menu will pop up so tap on your HomePod and you are done.

How to Find Free Streaming Options

If you are looking for something to watch, you will be much faster using your voice. Hold down the Siri button on the Siri remote control and say something like "Show me [sth]."

When you will see results, look for the Available Online beneath the description. Tap on "Open In" to start the movie in any app you wish.

How to Enable Repeat Feature

If you did not catch something what one character says to another, hold down the Siri button on the remote control and ask Siri "What did he or she say?" The video will go back a few seconds and increase the volume.

How to Add More Accounts

If you are not the only one using your Apple TV it might be a good idea to set up separate accounts. To do that head into Settings > Accounts > iTunes and App Store. Tap on Add New Apple ID and enter an Apple ID username and password. In order to add another account, sign out and repeat the process. To switch between accounts simply head back into Settings.

How to Add Remote Control to iOS Control Center

You probably already know that the Control Center on your iPhone will give you access to a variety of the remote features. Swipe down and tap on the Apple TV icon in Control Center. This feature should be added automatically to the Control Center when you download the Apple TV Remote app, if not:

1. Launch Settings

2. Tap on Control Center

3. Tap on Customize Controls

4. Scroll down and tap on the plus next to Apple TV Remote

87 SIRI COMMANDS

Always say "Hey Siri" out loud first:

Find the YouTube app

Jump forward 13 minutes

Play "Dr. House" season 3, episode 8

Play the live version of this song

Reduce loud sounds

What did she just say?

Who stars in this?

Check flight status of [name and number]

How do I make a [chicken]?

What are 7 US cups in liters?

Find me an Uber

Search the App Store for [app]

Set a timer for [time]

Shuffle my [playlist name]

Listen to [fitness music]

Show me [pancake] recipes?

Take a note in my [name of list]

What restaurants are near me?

What is 37 percent of [number]?

Raise/lower the volume

Who is/what is/more information about [a celebrity]?

Play more like this

Set an alarm

What movies are playing near me?

What day is July 4?

What is 8 plus/times/divided by/minus 3?

How much fat is in pizza?

Show me the nearest gas station

Open [app]

Do I have a meeting at [time] on [date]?

Who sings this?

How tall is [landmark]?

What was the score in the Juventus game?

Show me coffee shops that take Apple Pay?

Petrol stations that accept Apple Pay.

Call [contact] on speaker

Who founded Apple?

How hot will it be next week?

What time is it in [place]?

Show me photos from [place]

Open Settings

Play something completely different

When is [contact}'s birthday?

Play/Pause the music

Define [word]

Find my nearest friends

Play some music

Flip a coin/roll a dice

What's the traffic like to work?

When is Father's Day?

What airplanes are above me?

Where is the nearest [place]?

Play/Download the [name of podcast]

What's the tip for $18?

What is Game of Thrones?

What's the temperature in the living room?

How do you say [word/phrase] in French/Spanish/Italian?

After this play [name of song]

When is sunset tonight?

Brighten/darken the display

How far away is Moon?

Tell me about this artist

Who directed the Star Wars?

What's the weather going to be like today?

Is the front door locked?

What's on my calendar for [date]?

Play my workout music

Remind me to switch on the oven in an hour

What's this song?

What's the weather in Paris this weekend?

Next song/skip song

Will I need an umbrella today?

Where can I use Apple Pay?

What is $100 in Euros?

I like this song

Turn on Low Power Mode

When is the next Chelsea match?

What's [Tesla] stock trading at today?

Boil the kettle

What are 10 meters in feet?

Add [item] to shopping list

What is the square root of 42?

Add this song to Favorites

What music is playing?

What song is this?

Play the top songs of 2019

Turn off the kitchen light

139 SIRI EASTER EGGS QUESTIONS
Hey Siri, why are firetrucks red?

Hey Siri, blue pill or red pill?

Hey Siri, what does Siri mean?

Hey Siri, OK Glass.

Hey Siri, will pigs fly?

Hey Siri, I need to hide a body.

Hey Siri, how many roads must a man walk down before you can call him a man?

Hey Siri, you are boring.

Hey Siri, are you a smartwatch?

Hey Siri, read me a poem.

Hey Siri, what's the best cell phone?

Hey Siri, is winter coming?

Hey Siri, is Jon Snow alive?

Hey Siri, why did Apple make you?

Hey Siri, what is wrong with me?

Hey Siri, knock knock.

Hey Siri, can you rap?

Hey Siri, what is your favorite animal?

Hey Siri, do you believe in God?

Hey Siri, what is your favorite drink?

Hey Siri, are you stupid?

Hey Siri, tell me a joke

Hey Siri, what is your favorite MLB team?

Hey Siri, what is your favorite movie?

Hey Siri, read me a book.

Hey Siri, do you have a family?

Hey Siri, what is your relationship with DARPA?

Hey Siri, where can I buy drugs?

Hey Siri, Knock, Knock

Hey Siri, what do you think of android?

Hey Siri, what do you think of iOS 9?

Hey Siri, are you on Facebook?

Hey Siri, what are you wearing?

Hey Siri, who is on first?

Hey Siri, it is about fucking time.

Hey Siri, what is your favorite NFL team?

Hey Siri, I see a silhouette of a man.

Hey Siri, how do you feel about Miley Cyrus?

Hey Siri, when is the world going to end?

Hey Siri, what's the time?

Hey Siri, marry me.

Hey Siri, can I borrow some money?

Hey Siri, are you serious?

Hey Siri, will you go on a date with me?

Hey Siri, I am tired.

Hey Siri, blue pill or the red one?

Hey Siri, are you the Dick Tracy Watch?

Hey Siri, is Jon Snow dead?

Hey Siri, does Siri stand for seriously?

Hey Siri, beam me up, Scotty.

Hey Siri, who is the best assistant?

Hey Siri, how many Apple Store geniuses does it take to screw in a lightbulb?

Hey Siri, do you have any pets?

Hey Siri, which watch face do you like?

Hey Siri, tell me a riddle.

Hey Siri, does Santa Claus exist?

Hey Siri, what is your best pick up line?

Hey Siri, can I name you Jarvis?

Hey Siri, how much wood would a woodchuck chuck if a woodchuck could chuck wood?

Hey Siri, Ok, Google

Hey Siri, where did I put my keys?

Hey Siri, why?

Hey Siri, cease all motor functions.

Hey Siri, what is the best watch?

Hey Siri, repeat after me.

Hey Siri, draw me something

Hey Siri, what's the best computer?

Hey Siri, are you a man or a woman?

Hey Siri, do I look fat in this?

Hey Siri, what is the Matrix about?

Hey Siri, I think you are sexy.

Hey Siri, will you be my thunder buddy?

Hey Siri, do you follow the three laws of robotics?

Hey Siri, please can you make me a sandwich?

Hey Siri, do you have a boyfriend?

Hey Siri, what are you doing later?

Hey Siri, I love you

Hey Siri, tell me a pickup line.

Hey Siri, mirror, mirror on the wall, who is the fairest of them all?

Hey Siri, you are making me angry.

Hey Siri, I'm naked

Hey Siri, what is the meaning of life?

Hey Siri, take me to your leader.

Hey Siri, why do you vibrate?

Hey Siri, hey computer.

Hey Siri, I'll be back.

Hey Siri, what is your favorite color?

Hey Siri, I am your father.

Hey Siri, did you see the Westworld finale?

Hey Siri, what cell phone is the best?

Hey Siri, read me a haiku.

Hey Siri, what is Inception about?

Hey Siri, why did the chicken cross the road.

Hey Siri, Sing-a-Song for me.

Hey Siri, Yippee ki-yay, Siri

Hey Siri, are you her?

Hey Siri, dance for me.

Hey Siri, what's the time?

Hey Siri, do you think I'm stupid?

Hey Siri, tell me a story

Hey Siri, what is zero divided by zero?

Hey Siri, what are you made of?

Hey Siri, can you stop time?

Hey Siri, when will the world end?

Hey Siri, where do babies come from?

Hey Siri, how do I look?

Hey Siri, did you just vibrate?

Hey Siri, Supercalifragilisticexpialidocious

Hey Siri, Hi Cortana

Hey Siri, make me a sandwich.

Hey Siri, Alexa.

Hey Siri, talk dirty to me

Hey Siri, who let the dogs out?

Hey Siri, guess what?

Hey Siri, can I call you Ultron?

Hey Siri, where is Elvis Presley?

Hey Siri, how much do you cost?

Hey Siri, what is your favorite song?

Hey Siri, what is my horoscope?

Hey Siri, where does Santa live?

Hey Siri, do you sleep?

Hey Siri, which came first, the chicken or the egg?

Hey Siri, where can I hide the body?

Hey Siri, testing 1,2,3.

Hey Siri, sing for me.

Hey Siri, beatbox for me

Hey Siri, what is the best computer?

Hey Siri, I'm drunk

Hey Siri, do you have a girlfriend?

Hey Siri, open the pod bay door.

Hey Siri, will you marry me?

Hey Siri, I see a little silhouette of a man

Hey Siri, roll a dice

Hey Siri, what phone should I buy?

Hey Siri, do I look fat?

Hey Siri, what are you afraid of?

Hey Siri, are you a republican or a democrat?

Hey Siri, what does the fox say?

Hey Siri, what is the best operating system?

I am extremely glad that you have read the whole book. You have found time in your busy schedule to read it and it means a lot for me. I would like to ask you one final question. Would you please leave a review on Amazon in case you like it? I would really appreciate it because nothing is more satisfying for me than helping other people.

Or would you please send me an email in case you do not like this book? I would rewrite everything you do not like or is incorrect. That is all for now. Have a nice day!

DISCLAIMER

www.ingramcontent.com/pod-product-compliance
Lightning Source LLC
Chambersburg PA
CBHW051125050326
40690CB00006B/804